YOUR KNOWLEDGE HAS VALUE

Alex-Jean Kakule Mueni

Supply Chain Management. A discussion about managing supply chain risks

GRIN Verlag

Bibliografische Information der Deutschen Nationalbibliothek:

Die Deutsche Bibliothek verzeichnet diese Publikation in der Deutschen National-
bibliografie; detaillierte bibliografische Daten sind im Internet über http://dnb.d-
nb.de/ abrufbar.

Imprint:

Copyright © 2013 GRIN Verlag GmbH
Druck und Bindung: Books on Demand GmbH, Norderstedt Germany
ISBN: 978-3-656-63709-7

This book at GRIN:

http://www.grin.com/en/e-book/271487/supply-chain-management-a-discussion-
about-managing-supply-chain-risks

GRIN - Your knowledge has value

Der GRIN Verlag publiziert seit 1998 wissenschaftliche Arbeiten von Studenten, Hochschullehrern und anderen Akademikern als eBook und gedrucktes Buch. Die Verlagswebsite www.grin.com ist die ideale Plattform zur Veröffentlichung von Hausarbeiten, Abschlussarbeiten, wissenschaftlichen Aufsätzen, Dissertationen und Fachbüchern.

Visit us on the internet:

http://www.grin.com/

http://www.facebook.com/grincom

http://www.twitter.com/grin_com

Introduction:

In the past few years, we have witnessed several developments in each and every area of life. The development in the technology and introduction of new way outs have influenced all the areas of business and the supply chain of an organization as well. The markets are now not limited to the boundary of a single country but they are establishing themselves on a global level. Due to globalization, organizations have planned to redefine their supply chain management policies due to a huge incline in the demand and supply of products and services globally. Along with the profits to getting global, there are many risks faced by the supply chain of an organization. These risks can be man- made risks or natural calamities. Interruption in delivery of raw material, fluctuating prices in the market and rapid increase in the demand of the customer are also considered as supply chain risks. To operate the business effectively by delivering the product or service to the customers on right time and right place is the main goal of every business (Mentzer et al., 2001) To achieve this goal, a business should implement some strategies to manage the risk that are involved in the supply chain. There are many approaches suggested by the researches in order to manage and mitigate the supply chain risks. This paper is an attempt to gather knowledge about the approaches used in managing the supply chain risks. These approaches are discussed in this paper and a critical analysis of them is also conducted. In the end of this paper, some recommendations about the approaches is also given that may help in the future research of the risk management strategies.

Supply chain management:

The markets are going global, beyond the borders and they are re-defining the methods to manage the supply and demand of their products and services. Global companies are operating in the markets across continents. To keep the manufacturing cost low, these companies are looking forward to establish new production hubs where the raw material and labor are cheap.

Supply chain management (SCM) is to manage a network of interrelated businesses that are a part of providing products and services to the final consumers through a supply chain. The role of supply chain management in the company is to propose, plan, implement, govern, and monitor the activities relating to the supply chain activities. It involves all the

1

activities in managing and storing the raw material, inventory used in the work in process, finished goods and delivery it to the end consumer (Mentzer et al., 2001)

Risk:

The element of risk is present in each business activity and operation. In 2005, Kleindorfer and Saad stated in their paper that uncertainty in the political condition, eventualities in operations, terrorism and natural calamities and all such incidents are considered as s risk. Furthermore, all the natural and artificial catastrophes are the main causes of risk.

Risks in Supply Chain Management:

Like all other areas of business, supply chain of a company is also exposed to many risks. These risks can hinder the supply chain activities that results in a disruption in overall distribution network and the products and services are then unable to be delivered to the end consumer on right time and right place. The risks faced by the supply chains are of two types; external supply chain risks and internal supply chain risks. The external supply chain risk refers to the risks raised due to the up streaming or down streaming in a supply chain. The external supply chain risk includes demand risk; any unexpected demand from the consumers, supply risk; any disruption in the delivery of product or raw material through the distribution network, environmental risk; the risk that is beyond the supply chain that means any social, governmental policy or terrorism etc and business risk; instable financial condition of the supplier and risk of bankruptcy (Queensland government, 2013).

The internal supply chain risks are not considered as seriously as the external risks are considered. As the name shows that internal risks means the risks that are present in the internal operations of an organization so there are more chances to manage and lessen such risks as the management of the company has a control over them. The internal supply chain risks are risk in manufacturing of the product due to any interruption in the production process, inappropriate valuation and planning, managerial inefficiencies, cultural risks that means to delay the disclosure of any information that is not in the favor of the organization (Mand & Singh, 2013; Queensland government, 2013).

In his paper, Barry, J. (2004) proposed that risk in supply chain means the happening of such an incident that might slower down or break the flow of a supply chain. Furthermore, they stated that the supply risk is the possibility of occurrence of an event that is related to the failure of the incoming supply of the product by the supplier whether an individual or market and incapability of the buying company to meet the demands of the customers. According to them, the demand risk is the probability of a drastic change in the demand of the customer or demand fluctuations resulting in short product life cycle.

Supply Chain Risk Management:

Due to the unexpected trend in the demand and supply of the product, global outsourcing and limited product cycle, it is very challenging to manage the risks in such environmental situations (Abhijeet at al., 2012). At present, the business environment around the globe is effected by the inconsistency in the financial condition, in time contract out, mergers and acquisitions, new technological developments, e-business and less time span for a product to be in the market etc. as a result the companies are being induced to implement the new methods of conducting a business (Stefanovic et al, 2009).

On the other hand, the supply chain network of small and just-in-time globalized are considered to be facing greater risk than they were facing ever before because of internal and external interruptions. At present, Risk management is emerging as an essential measure of a holistic supply chain management design (Christopher and Lee, 2004; Bandaly et al,, 2013).

Supply chain risk management (SCRM) is the execution of certain policies in order to cope up with the routine risks and the unique risk in the supply chain by regular risk assessment with the main purpose to reduce the level of susceptibility and to ensure the stability of the supply chain (Palit et al., 2007).

Approaches to Supply Chain Risk Management:

As mentioned above in the paper, the supply chain has many risk associated with its activities. Such risks can cause severe damage to the whole distribution network. These risks do not result in a loss of a single party but all the stakeholders including the manufacturers, suppliers, wholesalers, retailers and ultimately the end customers who suffers because of not getting the required product or service in the right time. It is significant to manage the risk before it goes out of control. The risk is identified and assessed by an effective execution of the supply chain risk management policies.

There are then a variety of approaches present to manage and lessen the supply chain risk. Many scholars and researchers have shown their interest in this area mainly due to the complications and increased risk because of global outsourcing. They have conducted several researches to clarify the appropriate approach for supply chain risk management. Some of the approaches to supply chain risk management are discussed in detail below.

Managerial perception about risk:

The choice of right approach to manage the risk is very important and it is commonly decided by the behavioral aspect of the managers. A few researchers have conducted their research on the perceptions of managers about the risks in the supply chain. According to Zsidisin (2006), the decision of the managers to select any policy to tackle the risk whether it is to be risk averse, risk neutral, risk sharing or accepting or taking the risk, such behavior of the managers can directly impact the methods to mitigate the risk.

Collaborative Contracts Approach:

In the present era, companies are adopting the collaborative risk management approaches in the supply chain in order to share the risk and increase the possibility of success. The concept of globalized supply chain has increased the level of risk in the distribution network. Many researchers have proposed collaboration contracts as a long term and strong risk management approach in supply chain. In their research paper, Abhijeet st al., (2012), stated that risk can be shared by the collaboration contracts and out sourcing and it can increase the efficiency in the distribution network. Furthermore, they suggested that the strategic alliance between the partners and suppliers can prove helpful in mitigating and managing the risk in the supply chain. Due to the fluctuations in demand and price of a product, there is a probability of any uncertainty and the rising risk can be shared which will prove beneficial in handling the risk in supply chain in future time.

According to Mark Swabey (2010), there are several reasons of adopting a collaborative contact approach by the suppliers to handle the risk related to supply chain. He suggested that the collaboration of suppliers helps in identifying the risk more successfully, creating risk awareness, more possible way outs, more responsible monitoring and risk management and an effective risk mitigation strategy is implemented as a result of collaboration to tackle with it and the risk that is unavoidable is shared among the parries so that no party will suffer the greater portion of risk.

The change in the business environment has made the companies to concentrate more on coordination and collaborative strategies in order to minimize the risk within the distribution network in an effective manner than before (Piyush et al., 2011). Moreover, the research conducted by them also presents two models for collaborative business framework. The collaboration characterization model (CCM) is the first model described by them as an approach to manage the risk in supply chain is and the second model is collaboration oriented performance model (COP). The collaboration oriented performance model measures the performance of collaboration by the considering the elasticity, reactivity, and superiority of the supply chain (Cachon, 2003).

As per Cachon (2003), the concepts that are also considered by the researchers in reviewing the collaborative policies at functional and tactical level are the fluctuation and market instability, shorter life cycle of the product and unexpected demand by the consumers.

Visibility and Traceability Approach:

Piyush et al., (2011), also suggested that the availability of proper information is very significant in dealing with the risks related to the supply chain. It is claimed that the response to risk by an organization is effective if proper and updated information is provided. The new technologies will have a great effect in making the risk more visible within the supply chain so it can be managed in a better way.

Risk Propagation Approach:

In 2011, Alvarez suggested that risk profile and spreading risk models can help an organization in getting greater visibility in order to manage the risk more effectively. Additionally, to understand the possible limit to which risk can occur on the supply chain network gives new ideas to mitigate and propagate the risk. It can result in a better model used for management of risk. According to them, the planning of recovery from the aftershocks of risk has significance and for this purpose an adequate risk recovering strategy is needed with the help of sufficient information and involvement of the stakeholders.

There is a risk in the supply chain when the competitor is dealing better or doing such activities that influence the operations, when the customers and suppliers began to bargain more. To manage such risks, a suitable and operative organizational plan is needed. According to Peter finch (2004), an organization can use an approach of re-organizing its supply chain management strategies to alleviate this risk.

As per Alicke et al., (2011), some companies that have been imposed to implement the predetermined risk management strategies are witnessing gaps and instability in their approaches to manage the supply chain risk. In addition, they suggested that such companies should upgrade their approaches to risk management and this is the actual approach to rectify the supply chain risk. The key feature that should be added in the future risk management strategy should be an incline in the flexibility of the supply chain. They have recommended an approach of three levels. The first step is to identify the risk and its effects on the supply chain, next to it is to design, adopt and monitor the risk mitigation strategies and the lase step is the most important for the above mentioned companies and it is to make sure that the implemented strategies are updated and integrated with the business operations with the passage of time (Alicke, Zerlin, & Wente, 2011).

Sometimes a risk appears in the supply chain when the supplier is new or when the purchased product is expensive and there is a risk of damage to the product while delivery. There are four dimensions that should be defined to get an appropriate approach to manage this supply chain risk. These dimensions includes to determine the level of technology of purchased product, level of security in managing, storing and transporting the product, significance of the supplier whether regular or one time supplier and past purchasing experience to buy the product from the supplier or it is being purchased for the first time (Larry et al., 2004).

Knowledge Based Management Approach:

In the environment where the businesses are knowledge driven, it is felt necessary to use the knowledge based management approaches to supply chain risk management. An organization can use unconventional knowledge, communication technology and other tools of knowledge based management in order to get a competitive advantage, mostly while dealing with a multifaceted range of risks within the supply chain (Solomon, Ketikidis, & Choudhary, 2012).

Though, Solomon et al., (2012), have emphasized on two major agendas that are risk management and knowledge management. These two models have a limitation that the quantitative data is not amply tested.

Real Option Approach:

According to Cohen & Huchzermeier (1999), the level of suppleness is increased in the supply chain since the real options strategy is been introduced. It can assist a lot in recovering the effects of market fluctuations. They explained in their paper that the damages due to the risk in the demand of the product by the customers resulting in a rapid change in trend and fluctuations in exchange rate and price of the product can be controlled to an extend by applying the real option theory.

Many researchers like Federica and Massimo (2006) also conducted a research on the real option theory. They revealed that in case when the investments in the supply chain have been made in an unsecured business environment, the real option theory suggests the adaptation of the right policy in accordance with the situation and these chosen policies also assist in making the production process more flexible. The more the business environment is uncertain, the more probability of success is there for the real option theory (Federica, Massimo, 2006).

Robust Optimization and Worst-Case Scenario Approaches:

Another approach to manage the supply chain risk is the robust optimization that is to overview such indoctrination emphasized on optimality and possibility of the way out (Mulvey et al., 1995). In contrary to this approach, another approach was proposed in the research paper by Hahn & H.Kuhn in 2012. This approach was not considering the ideal conditions but the worst case scenrios. The robust optimization model was also discussed in his research paper and he claimed that the risk averse approach is a feature of optimization theory.

According to Hadavale et al.(2009), there are three interconnected approaches that provide new perceptions to manage the risk in supply chains. These three approaches include supply network design, supplier relationship and supplier selection. The supply network design approach reflects the functioning limits over interruption risks and flexibility in the supply chain is considered significant in this approach. The supplier relationship approach is changed a bit to a supportive approach and it considers the transactions and adjustments between the long term and short term supply relationship. The last strategy is the supplier selection approach, it deals with the criteria on which the suppliers are selected and further process is preceded. Due to the capability of capturing any inconsistency in the performance and behavior of the supplier, the risk based supplier selection models are getting more attention at present but such approach needs more consideration explicitly in disorderly risk when there are many alternative measure of performance like recovery period (Hadavale, S, Alexander, & M, 2009).

Holistic approach:

A complete and Holistic approach for supply chain risk management is not exactly found in the present literature. Every approach has its flaws and up gradation and integration is required for all. According to White (2010), a perfect approach for supply chain risk management is needed that will provide new ideas to solve the present risks in the supply chain and to be further utilized in tackling the future uncertainties. An incorporated method for supply chain risk management is required to fit in the problems regarding the risks in practical industry. The researchers are carrying out further researches to redesign and integrate some approaches to structure a complete supply chain risk management approach for the current indeterminate and dynamic surroundings (Stadtler, 2005).

Risk management approaches:

In 2010, Taticchi proposed that it is a critical job to execute a supply chain risk management strategy as it requires the proper information related to the operations of the business, current trends in the market and economic and infrastructural position of the organization and the whole supply chain as well. He suggested three general steps to execute a supply chain risk management strategy which includes detecting the risks faced by the organization, weighing the risks and its consequences and implementing an appropriate risk management approach. An order is present between these stages and the higher stage incorporates the lower stage (Taticchi, 2010).

As risk detection is a first and the most important step in risk management, there are many approaches suggested in the literature to identify the potential risks. Some of the several strategies to identify the supply chain risk include common listing approach; previous data is used to get idea about the future risks, taxonomy based approach; framework to bring out and form actions to detect the risk in the business operations, scenario analysis; considering different situations to plan their consequences on the supply chain and to analyze the performance and design plans to mitigate the risk at functional level and risk mapping; competent to expose the susceptibility within the supply chains to possible risk before their existence. Risk classification approach is also helpful and provides a comprehensive structure to assess the risk.

Piyush et al., (2011) also proposed that there are three approaches to manage the risk in the operations of the company. These three approaches are categorized as risk shaper, risk accepter and risk recovery. To reduce the effect and occurrence of risk without making any change in the supply chain is risk shaper approach, the risk accepter approach accepts the risk in the supply chain and then the supply chain is restructured. The risk recovery approach attempts to implement policies to recover the damages after the occurrence of any uncertainty.

Some researches present risk management approaches like avoid risk, reduce risk, transfer risk or accept risk to manage the supply chain risk (McCormack, 2008; Norrman, 2004).

According to Kaipia (2004), suggested different tools that should be implemented to manage the risks involved in the supply chain process. These tools are materials flow, information flow and cost and performance.

Information flow is the proper flow of information between the suppliers in the supply chain. To smooth out materials flow, there should be proper and clear selection and assortment of products. Cost and performance assessment refers to the assessment of the overall cost and performance of the product, supplier and customers as well (Lia et al., 2004).

Critical analysis:

By going through the literature on supply chain risk management, it is found that it is really important to recover the issues regarding the interruptions in the demand and supply of goods and services. The management behavior perspective impacts the method to manage the supply chain risk. Collaboration contracts and alliances between the suppliers are and effective and promising approach to manage, monitor and share the risk within the supply chain. A proper coordination within the suppliers can assist in reducing the degree of uncertainty in the supply chain network and strengthens the distribution chain. It is analyzed that the main purpose of collaboration contracts is to manage the uncertain condition and the existing collaboration tools can be revised considering the potential risks. The identification of risk is only possible if there is appropriate information available. Knowledge based management approach is grounded on the proper availability of information about all the activities involved in the supply chain but the risk management will be resulted in failure if there is any flaw in the provided information. During the analysis of the literature it is found that the element of flexibility in supply chain is essential in the recovery planning of the risk. It is examined that the visibility of risk impacts the alliance between the suppliers. Scenario based approach is not considered as suitable as they consider the worst case or the optimal case and the reality may not be as they consider it. It is investigated that if the past information about risk is available then risk shaper policies are considered to be best to manage the situation and when the risks are inevitable, it is wise to accept the risk and implement policies to redesign the supply chain structure and then approaches to recover the risk are executed.

Conclusion and Recommendations:

The markets are globalized and they are re-defining their supply chain structure to fulfill the increased demand and supply of the product. The supply chain is exposed to more risks and uncertainties after being globalized. While analyzing the above literature, it is conclude that it is significant to manage the supply chain risk in order to operate effectively. Several approaches are proposed by the researchers to manage the supply chain risk. The collaboration between the supplier helps in managing the risk more quickly and efficiently. Risk identification is a noteworthy step in managing the risk.

The approaches to supply chain risk management should be up graded and integrated with the passage of time. It is recommended that the firms should not adopt the pre-determined policies to manage the supply chain risk. There should be an up gradation in the policies by perceiving the potential risks. It was apparent during the analysis of the literature that research in many areas is needed. The default risk of supplier, risk related to the quality and management in the supply chain are the major areas that are unexplored (Stadtler, 2005). There is insufficient research work done related to the propagation of risk. A holistic supply chain management approach is missing. The multidimensional viewpoint emphasizing on the managerial procedures, risk magnitudes, impact movements and substitute to mitigation policies is required. It is suggested to conduct a further research in which all the stakeholders and their connections to the supply chain should be considered in recognizing the risks and uncertainties to the supply chain network.

References:

Abhijeet Ghadge, Samir Dani, Roy Kalawsky, (2012) "Supply chain risk management: present and future scope", International Journal of Logistics Management, The, Vol. 23 Iss: 3, pp.313 - 339

Alicke, K., Zerlin, B., & Wente, I. M. (2011). A NEW APPROACH TO SUPPLY CHAIN RISK MANAGEMENT. *Supply Chain Europe* , 10-11.

Alvarez, G. (2011). Sustainability and Quality: The creation and operation of multistakeholder networks in ethical supply chains. *Cranfield School of Management, Executive DBA Student, Cranfield University.*

Bandaly, D., Shanker, L., Kahyaoglu, Y., & Satir, A. (2013). Supply chain risk management – II: A review of operational, financial and integrated approaches.

Barry, J. (2004). Supply chain risk in an uncertain global supply chain environment. *International Journal of Physical Distribution & Logistics Management, 34*(9), 695 - 697.

Cachon, G.P. (2003). Supply Chain Coordination with Contracts, 3rd draft, in *Handbooks in Operations Research and Management Science: Supply Chain Management, (*S. Graves and T. de Kok, eds.), North-Holland, Holland.

Cohen, M.A. and Huchzermeier, A. (1999), "Global supply chain management: a survey of research and applications", in Tayur, S. and Ganeshan, R. (Eds), Quantitative Models for Supply Chain Management, Kluwer, Boston, MA, pp. 669-702.

Federica Cucchiella, Massimo Gastaldi, (2006) "Risk management in supply chain: a real option approach", Journal of Manufacturing Technology Management, Vol. 17 Iss: 6, pp.700 - 720

Hahn, G., & H.Kuhn. (2012). Value-basedperformanceandriskmanagementinsupplychains:. *International Journal of Production Economics*, 135-144.

Hadavale, S, R., Alexander, & M, S. (2009). Supply Chain Risk Management. *IIE Annual Conference. Proceedings*, 1363-1368.

Kaipia, R. (2004). COORDINATING MATERIAL AND INFORMATION FLOWS.

Kleindorfer, P. R., & Saad, G. H. (2005). Managing Disruption Risks in Supply Chains. *Production and Operation Management Vol. 14, No. 1,*, 53-68.

Larry C. Giunipero, Reham Aly Eltantawy, (2004) "Securing the upstream supply chain: a risk management approach", International Journal of Physical Distribution & Logistics Management, Vol. 34 Iss: 9, pp.698 – 713

Lia, S., Ragu-Nathanb, B., Ragu-Nathanb, T., & Raob, S. S. (2004). The impact of supplychain management practices on competitive advantage and organizational performance.

Mand, J. S., Singh, C. D., & Singh1, R. (2013). IMPLEMENTATION OF CRITICAL RISK FACTORS IN SUPPLY CHAIN MANAGEMENT. *International Journal of management research and business strategy.*

Mark Swabey. *(2010)*. Collaborative Risk Management. [Online] Available at: http://www.riskreasoning.co.uk/filer.cfm?file=collaborative_risk [Accessed 29 April 2013].

Martin Christopher, Hau Lee, (2004) "Mitigating supply chain risk through improved confidence", International Journal of Physical Distribution & Logistics Management, Vol. 34 Iss: 5, pp.388 – 396

McCormack, D. K. (2008). Managing Risk in Your Organization with the SCOR Methodology. *The Supply Chain Council Risk Research Team.*

Mentzer, J. T., DeWitt, W., Keebler, J. S., & Min, S. (2001). Defining supply chain management. *Journal of Business Logistics, 22*(2), 1-25.

Mukaddes, A. M., Rashed, C. A., Malek, A. B., & Javed. (2010). Developing an Information Model for Supply Chain Information Flow and its Management. *International Journal of Innovation, Management and Technology, Vol. 1, No. 2.*

Mulvey, J. M., Vanderbei, R. 1., & Zenios, S. A. (Mar. - Apr., 1995). Robust Optimization of Large-Scale Systems. *Operations Research, Vol. 43, No.2,* 264-281

Norrman, A. (2004). Ericsson's proactive supply chain risk management approach after a serious sub-supplier accident. *Department of Industrial Management and Logistics, Lund University.*

Palit, A., Joshi, R., Narvekar, R., & Rastogi, G. (2007). Supply Chain Management: New Trends And Strategies .

Peter Finch, (2004) "Supply chain risk management", Supply Chain Management: An International Journal, Vol. 9 Iss: 2, pp.183 – 196

Queensland government.(2013). Identifying supply chain risks. [Online] Available at: http://www.business.qld.gov.au/business/running/risk-management/managing-risks-supply-chains/identifying-supply-chain-risks [Accessed 29 April 2013].

Simchi-Levi, D., Kaminsky, P. and Simchi-Levi, E. (2008). *Designing and Managing the Supply Chain: Concepts, Strategies and Case Studies.* McGraw-Hill/Irwin, New York.

Solomon, A., Ketikidis, P., & Choudhary, A. (2012). A Knowledge Based Approach for Handling Supply Chain.

Stadtler, H. (2005). Invited review. Supply chain management and advanced planning basics, overview and challenges, *European Journal of Operational Research.,* 163:575-588.

Stefanović, N., & Stefanović, D. (2012). Supply Chain Performance Measurement System Based on Scorecards and Web Portals. *Faculty of Science, University of Kragujevac, Radoja Domanovica.*

Taticchi, P. (2010). *Business Performance Measurement and Management: New Contents, Themes and Challenges.* Springer.

Vanany, I., Zailani, S., & Pujawan, N. (2009). Supply Chain Risk Management: Literature Review and Future Research. *International Journal of Information Systems and Supply Chain Management, 2(1)*, 16-33.

White, L. (2010). Operational research and sustainable development: Tackling the social dimension, *European Journal of Operational Research.*, 193:683-692.

Zsidisin, G. (2006). Managerial Perceptions of Supply Risk. *Journal of Supply Chain Management.*